Writing Articles and Books for Publications

About the Author

Prof. G. Palanithurai, Former Professor, Rajiv Gandhi Chair for Panchayati Raj studies, Department of Political Science and Development Administration, Gandhigram Rural Institute – Deemed University, Gandhigram is an academic activist. All his academic, research and outreach activities are being supported by an array of funding agencies, namely the world Bank, UNDP, UNICEF, Hunger Project, SDC, DANIDA, Action Aid International, Ford Foundation, Population Foundation of India, Rajiv Gandhi Foundation, Toolkit Foundation Netherland, Ministry of Panchayati Raj and State Planning Commission. He was a visiting professor in Cologne University, Germany. He has to his credit seventy three books, 126 research articles, 112 popular articles in popular newspapers, 83 monographs published in a span of three decades. He was and is member of many advisory committees of the Government of India and Government of Tamil Nadu pertinent to local governance and rural development.

Writing Articles and Books for Publications

G. Palanithurai

CONCEPT PUBLISHING COMPANY PVT. LTD.
NEW DELHI-110059

ISBN: 978-93-86682-59-8 (HB)
ISBN: 978-93-86682-60-4 (PB)

First Published 2024

Published and Printed by

Concept
Since 1974

Concept Publishing Company Pvt. Ltd.
A/15-16, Commercial Block, Mohan Garden,
New Delhi-110059 (India)
T : +91-11-41101460
E : publishing@conceptpub.com, *W* : www.conceptpub.com

Cataloging in Publication--Courtesy: D.K. Agencies (P) Ltd. <docinfo@dkagencies.com>

Palanithurai, G., author.
Writing articles and books for publication / G. Palanithurai.
pages cm
Includes index.
ISBN 9789386682598 (HB)
ISBN 9789386682604 (PB)

1. Authorship. 2. Creative writing. I. Title.

LCC PN145.P35 2024 | DDC 808.02 23

TO

THE DIVINE MOTHER

This monograph is prepared for young Social Science and Humanities scholars and not for pure Science scholars.

I have written this book not because no other competent person is in the field but no other individual has come forward to do such a kind of work for the benefit of young scholars emerging from obscurity. The whole exercise is purely based on my experience.

How to Read this Small Motivator?

It is not a guide
Or a manual but
it is a motivator
if you decide to write
please read. When
you read left side of
every page you find
principles, steps and
keys. On the right
side of every page
details are written
in boxes. It is written not
for examination purpose.
When you complete this
motivator, select one
model write up or
article from a reputed journal
or report and keep
it with you for reference and
start writing. It will be
a struggle in the beginning and
after some time it will be joyful.

Write Write Write

Preface

In emerging and challenging world, we want more number of well qualified social science researchers to do research in the field of social science as social, economic, political problems are more complicated and intense because of the advent of globalization and decentralization. The Indian higher education scenario gives a grim picture about the condition of Social Science Research. Science and Technology have gone to the market mode which drives the society as consumers. In the consumerist world, consumption and profit become the prime movers. As a result, society has to face volley of problems which are complicated in nature. To tackle the intense and complicated social problems, we need well qualified researchers. Students coming out of schools prefer to go to either Medicine, or Engineering or any skill related programmes which fetches lucrative jobs. In Tamil Nadu alone 50 per cent of the students coming from the schools after passing out of +2, are joining only Medicine and Engineering Programmes. Ten years back it was only 15 per cent and now it has gone to 50 per cent. Rarely students join Social Science programmes. The students who are joining the Social Science programmes are below average. Only a few who are well qualified joining in Social Science programme are only in premier institutions. Getting qualified students to Social Science programmes of the colleges and universities is very difficult. Further even if more number of students are joining, preparing them for research is difficult as the teachers in the Social Science faculties are not performing their tasks professionally. 80 per cent of the teachers are not active researchers and effective writers and communicators. Many assessment reports have indicated the poor quality of research and teaching of Social Science disciplines. In this context mobilizing students for Social Science programmes and preparing them for Social Science research are imperative needs. At the same time preparing the faculty for quality research and quality teaching is yet another stupendous task.

The UGC is continuously taking steps to strengthen quality research and yet needed momentum is not picking up. In this context I am joining with many to prepare younger researchers and scholars for quality research on critical areas and critical issues. I am joining with some of the colleges and civil society organizations in conducting series of preparatory training programmes for the newly recruited teachers and senior research scholars. After conducting a few programmes, I have been asked some of the participants to publish what I have presented in the training programmes and workshops. Hence, I made this attempt. There are many such books available in the market. But they are of high standard. What we want to do is to prepare an ordinary person with poor socio-economic background for intensive social science action research. Our intension is to prepare scholars from the affected communities to do research on the issues which affect them. In 2009 I visited Senegal to participate in a workshop I found interesting academic activities of some of the Academic Foundations with liberal funding of some of the agencies. They were preparing the young black scholars to do action research on the issues affecting the African Countries. When I interacted with them, they told me that they did not want anybody coming from West and do research on the problems of Africa. In this context they were preparing young black scholars. This motivated me to do this exercise.

Against this backdrop, I have prepared this monograph. I am convinced that I have to prepare this monograph in a simplest way so that I can make and motivate the students passing out from the Social Science programmes to undertake research on the critical issues which affected their own community. For this exercise, I have been motivated by Father Dr. Maria Joseph Mahalingam of Loyola College of Chennai. In fact he is organizing such kind of programmes periodically. In the same way there is yet another organization functioning in Madurai called "Evidence". This organization is conducting series of action research programmes on the issues of Dalit and the organization is preparing reports for policy advocacy. I use the data generated by this organization for my academic writings. I closely interact with the Director of the organization Mr. Kadhir. There is yet another organization EKTA a women resource centre working for women empowerment. This organization recruits sensitive students from Universities and trains them in action research. Further they do conduct action research and prepare reports for policy advocacy. I closely move with them. Likewise many organizations need such a kind of support. The above mentioned organizations are doing extremely well compared to traditional universities in this area. I move with them, interact with them and work with them. In this context I have to thank a few who are really the motivating individuals to do this exercise. They are Dr. Maria Joseph Mahalingam, Mr. Khadir of Evidence and Mrs. Bimla Chandrasekar of EKTA. I have prepared lectures for the programmes in Loyola College and the same are being used for this monograph. I thank my staff and project staff along with my family members for having stood with me for all my academic endeavours.

G. Palanithurai

Contents

I
Introduction

In India, social science research is not in expected standard. I have seen the report of social science research in the world, report of social science research in south Asia and report of social science research in India. Along with report of Knowledge Commission, report of UGC, report of Indian Council of Social Science Research many of independent research reports have been perused by me. From all the reports primarily I have gained two main points. They are: (i) only a smaller segment of the teachers in higher learning institutions are doing research continuously and publishing; and (ii) even the published materials based on the research conducted are not of high quality. In this context one has to take note of series of measures to improve the quality of teaching and research. Capacity building exercises have been conducted continuously in the universities. Further, it has been made mandatory for the teachers in higher learning institutions that publication of articles and books is necessary for promotion in their career from one level to next. Apart from the above, for Ph.D. and M.Phil. programmes course work is made mandatory. Further enabling conditions have been created by providing publication grant to the teachers and by which teachers are encouraged to publish articles and books. One set of teachers out of passion, curiosity and interest continuously pursuing research, publish papers in refereed journals and books through reputed publishers. Others continuously take classes for students and publish a few for promotion and spent the rest of the time as they like. Against this background some of institutions are taking earnest interest to promote a research culture. The institutions are concentrating on the newly recruited staff.

Loyola is one among a few taking serious interest in building a research culture among the staff. Though it is a college, it is doing the function of an university. Periodically, they organise programme for young scholars on how to write books, how to write articles and how to prepare research proposals for project. For all the programmes Loyola College invited reputed scholars from social science. I was invited continuously for this programme. I delivered lectures to the participants, along with other scholars from IIT and Business schools. I accept the invitation of Loyola College because of the commitment with which they organize programmes. All the presentations made in Loyola College have been given in this monograph.

The difficult task is to decide to write. It is not as you are going to the market for shopping. It is a determination. It is a struggle. Whether it is popular writing, or research writing, writing needs commitment, love, passion and joy. Especially for the academics, it is a mandate but in Indian setting it is not pursued seriously. Once in a while teachers in the higher educational institutions write articles for career advancement as it is stipulated by the UGC. What we aim here is to sensitise the teacher to do research. The teachers in higher educational institution have to be experts and professionals and for which they have to work on an important area and on a mission mode. Such individuals have to decide on to whom they are writing. Some teachers strongly argue that they are basically researchers and hence they will write only research articles. They won't do more beyond it. Some use to argue that they will write research articles and based on the research articles they write popular article for dissemination. Further, they will take it to policy advocacy also. All the three are difficult though on the same theme.

One should have passion for doing research and writing articles, monographs, working papers and books. In Indian context, it is an imperative if one wants to thrive in academic journey. Hence, it is necessary to motivate the academics to do research and write articles and books. If a teacher wants to be evolving throughout the career he or she has to do research, teach and outreach through actions. A teacher has to connect himself or herself with his/her clients, namely the students, the communities in which he/she works and policy makers pertinent to the issues. If a newly recruited Assistant Professor selects an issue and works for ten years on the same issue, he/she will be an expert in the field in the rest of his career and for which he has to do research and write articles, reports, monographs, working papers and books. First step is to have determination to write. Once the individual has decided to remain an active and inevitable teacher; he/she has to be in all the three domains of higher educational institutions, namely teaching, research and outreach or extension activities. To be precise on the three domains, the teacher has to select an area for his/her specialization. Precisely, Ph.D. is a starting point. If he/she is not able to fix the area from the Ph.D. research, at least after joining the academic or research institution, he/she has to fix the area. Once the area is fixed, the scholar has to establish his/her grip over the area by a strenuous reading of related literature. The domain reading of books and articles will give the scholar fair idea of the subject wherefrom all kinds of investigations will start. How to start, how to proceed and how to sustain in research and publication will be discussed in this monograph.

II
Decision to Write

Decide, why you want to write	You will be driven always by your decision
Your Writing depends on your goal	Nature and scope of writing will be determined by your goal

Purpose and category of writing	To become a specialist To bring new addition to existing knowledge To create new Knowledge To contest the existing knowledge	You have to write Research Article and Books
	To do policy advocacy	You have to write Reports for Advocacy
	To mobilize people To popularize ideas To sensitize people	You have to write popular Articles

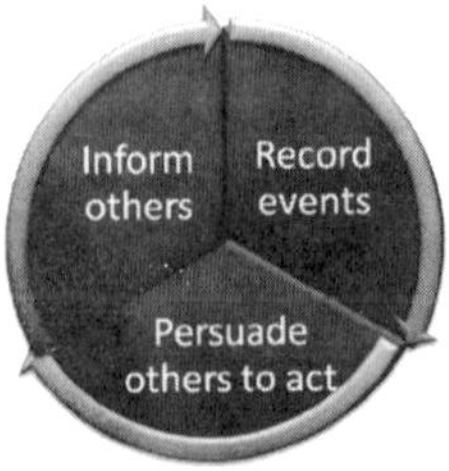

Ultimately there are three objectives behind writings. To inform others what we know one has to write. To register events either for present analysis or mere for the sake of history one has to write. Sometimes to persuade one to act one has to write. Essentially three objectives are behind writing.

III
Basic Steps

Basic Steps	
Need	There should be a felt need. It may be from outside or in you. You are asked to produce evidence of publication for promotion and for which you have to publish papers and books. When many teachers are doing project in your department, it will create a feeling that you will be considered either lazy or incompetent and hence you will be compelled to do research and publish. If you do project, you generate data, and you make analysis. Hence, you will be tempted to write and publish articles and books.
Faith	You should have faith in what you do. Unless you have faith in you, you cannot do any work. Faith in you is the basic fact to motivate a person. I have seen many intelligent teachers have not published much. When I make analysis based on my interaction with them, I found that they lack faith in them. I have seen many who are struggling to publish and they publish also. Self-motivation is the basic ingredient for making many to work.

Plan	Everything needs a plan—Neatly chalked out plan. Whether to write a popular article or research article or book, or a monograph or a working paper, it requires a meticulous planning. Just like a product it will come out and for which planning is an essential step.
Hard work	Hard work is one of the most important elements to bring success. There is no substitute to hard work. Hard work brings results and achievement in all our actions. So one has to prepare himself or herself for hard work.
System	System alone will bring regularity. It should be in your house or in your office. It is nothing but mere arrangements. It is nothing but doing things systematically, keeping things systematically and thinking systematically. System brings huge success. One can feel this result when one develops systems for their thinking and action.

IV
By Writing

You are visible

By writing articles in journals, by writing books, by writing reports, by writing popular articles you will be able to reach out to millions. By doing so you are visible. You are visible to millions and millions of people.

You are known

You are visible and it brings contacts for many purposes. By your continuous writing and contributions you will be familiar to many. In a particular area of specialisation or subject you are a familiar person among the peer group in the subject.

You are connected

You will be connected to the academic world very quickly. Your connection will go beyond your town and university. When your academic contributions grow your contacts with outside world will also grow. You are well connected and it brings several things to you.

You are wanted

You will be wanted for higher academic world for higher academic activities, Policy advocacy, Knowledge generations and disseminations. You will be sought. You will be on high demand.

You are criticized

Equally you will be criticized. Constructive criticism will be always stepping stones for your furtherance of activities in the academic domain. You gain further visibility. You are visible by being criticized.

You are appreciated	Your articles and books will be quoted by many. Through citation index you will be further recognized. When you bring credits to the institution where you work your institutional head will appreciate you. People will review your work.
You are rewarded	Rewards are of many types. You will get invitation from various institutions for academic assignments. You can get assignment aboard. When your mobility is increased your income will also be increased. You will get consultancy. You will get projects.
You are respected	When you are a most sought after person you will be a respectable person where you are working. Your respectability rate will be increased further. To lead a honest, active academic life writing is the most basic act for an academician in higher learning institutions.
Are you going loose anything?	You are not loosing anything. Instead you are gaining many things. One can lead a enjoyable, productive and fruitful life in the academic world by writing and publishing.
You will become popular	You are popular among the stakeholders and readers. Your popularity and familiarity will grow steadily. You will be a recognized person since you are a learned person.
You are the most demanded person	Once you reach certain stage in the knowledge domain is a particular area, you are the most sought after person. Your expert opinion is sought for everything.
You are connected regionally, nationally, and internationally	You will become a well-connected person regionally, nationally and internationally. Only through your publications, you will continue to receive invitation from everywhere.

The entire higher education system will be improved	If teachers in higher learning institution are publishing the whole system of higher education will be improved. Because knowledge enhancement will take place.
Quality of education will be improved	Quality of teaching will be improved enormously, if the teachers in higher learning institutions are doing research continuously and publishing papers continuously.
Economy will be improved	You are gaining money also. If you are a specialist you will be a consultant, by doing project, you will be paid extra. Consultants and advisers are earning money apart from salary.
Thus publishing is for our sake, for our country sake and for our people's sake	It is for you, for your society, for your country. When you do it with a sense of commitment and responsibility, you will be remembered for ever.

V
Through Publication

Name registered	Your name will be registered on an area where you are contributing much through your writing. But it requires specialization. You have to write continuously on the theme you have chosen.
Become a specialist	You are not an ordinary person. You are a specialist like an ortho doctor. You are a specialist in livelihood or poverty analysis or policy analysis. You will become specialist only when you deeply concentrate on a particular subject through your writing.
You can earn money	By writing articles, and books you can earn money. When you are invited for consultancy, you can earn money. When you get invitation from foreign countries, your earning will be doubled. By publishing books you can get royalty.
You can get constantly	You will be always on sky. As you get invitation and assignment from various organisations and institutions. For presentation or consultancy, you will travel widely and by which your visibility is increased.
You will get foreign assignment	Your writing alone increase your visibility. Academics are known only through their writings. In social science one can get easily foreign assignment if they become specialist through continuous writing on issues.

You are an inevitable person	If you are writing based on your research for a long on a particular area then you are an inevitable person. When you become inevitable person you cannot be ignored. You will be always in the limelight. You will be continuously invited for expert opinion.
You will be in committees and commissions	Governments both centre and state constitute committees and commissions periodically and you will be invited to become member of many committees and commissions.

VI
Significance of Publishing Articles in Journals

A knowledgeable society is a developed society	If a society wants to be a developed society, it should be a knowledgeable society. Knowledge is created through a systematic examination.
A developed society witnesses the higher level of human activities	Higher level of human actions indicates the level of the society. Higher level of human action is based on the higher level of knowledge.
Being a teacher she/he has to do research, teach and disseminate what she/he has created	Knowledge is produced only by the scientists and intellectuals in the higher learning institutions in a systematic way. Generate knowledge and disseminate the same through outreach programmes.
A teaching is connecting himself/herself with the stakeholders by teaching and writing articles in the journals	When you write articles or books you are connected with outside world and through your ideas you are influencing the society. You make opinion and create ideas and through which you are influencing the society.
Teaching, research and outreach are the basic responsibilities of a teacher in the colleges and universities	Writing is basic for a teacher in a Higher learning institution and by which they reach out to all stakeholders. Your teaching ability and skill will be enhanced if you write continuously.
While publishing our contributions knowledge generated are being disseminated	Generated knowledge has to be disseminated through publishing. Dissemination process takes place only through your writing.

You are connecting yourself with others working in the field	You are well connected, widely connected and you are always in contact with outside world.
You are gaining visibility	You are visible, you are known, and you are well connected. You are identified and you are the sought after person.
You are contesting the existing arguments	While writing you are contesting the existing knowledge.
You are creating new knowledge	You are creating a new knowledge on a particular area. You are a creator of knowledge. You are a creator of ideas. You are an innovator of a tool in methodology.
By doing so you are moving up on the knowledge ladder	By writing articles and books you are moving up in knowledge ladder. Number of publications and their quality will determine the space for you.
By doing so you are a specific person	When you write article and books, you are always known with specialization. You will be identified with your specialization. You have distinct identity and it is created by you.
By doing so you are known for your contribution	Your contribution will speak for you. You will be taken to different places by your articles and books. It is your creation and hence you can be proud of yourself.
	By publishing articles, books, monographs and working papers you will be connected with the world, you are recognized and you make resources also. You will be the most sought after person. You will get adequate material rewards also.

> If you are a teacher in a higher learning institution, you have three mandated functions or responsibilities. They are teaching, Research and Extension or Outreach. All the responsibilities have to be carried out by adopting golden mean formula. To do of all the three functions publications are imperative need.

VII
Research Writing

Specific problem Identification	Researcher should have a clear formulation of a problem to be investigated. The whole investigation depends on the way in which problem is formulated. It requires much clarity and much precision.
Either from the society or from theory	Many of the occasions researcher formulates research problem from the society as they confront it or from theory. While looking at the problems in the society, the researcher is tempted to take up for investigation.
Proper conceptualization	Once a problem is formulated, it is to be conceptualized for proper investigation. Conceptual clarity will enable the investigators to pursue research more easily.
Theoretical framework for guidance	Theory is always a guide post. It sheds light on the problem and through theory one can investigate the problem scientifically. Research base will be very sound if research is pursued in the backdrop of a theory.
Tracing the issue historically	While investigating any problem, it has to be seen in context and at the same time it has to be seen in historical perspective. Historical perspective will give the background of the issues. It forms the setting of the report or book or article.

Issues have to be looked at from perspectives	Perspectives are more important. Some look at issues from Gandhian perspective or Ambedkar perspective or Marxian perspective, or Periyar perspective, or environmental perspective and so on. Perspective is a lens to look at issues.
Relevant approach has to be used	Approach is also important for any investigation. Some look at issues from the historical approach or contemporary approach or contextual and so on. Approach will enable you to analyse the issues meticulously.
Appropriate theoretical arguments have to be used	For any investigation role of theory is an imperative one as it gives direction or clarity to the process investigation. Apart from the above, to interpret and explain the results theoretical arguments are needed.
Contextually the issue has to be analysed	Contextual analysis will give the correct background of the issues.
Relevant data have to be generated	The relevant data pertinent to the problem have to be collected. Proper conceptualization will enable you to collect only relevant information.
Appropriate tools for analysis have to be indentified	Data have to be classified into quantitative and qualitative and appropriate tools of analysis have to be identified. With the indentified tools data have to be analysed.
Results interpreted	Once the results are obtained out of analysis, they are to be interpreted after testing the hypotheses. Each and every aspect has to be explained. Explanation and interpretation give life to the results. Researcher has to make the results to speak.
Conclusion drawn	Finally, conclusions are to be drawn from the interpretation and explanation. It is process of distillation from explanation and arguements.

VIII

Once Decided to Write on a Subject

Start Reading	Vast reading is the basic need for any writing. Proper understanding of the subject and issue will enable the individual to look at problems in perspective. Broader reading will enable the researcher to move deeper into the issues.
Trace the Issue	Precise formulation of problem will lead the individual to investigate the same thoroughly and meticulously. If you have vast reading, the problem under investigator should be in the background of the history.
Think of Theory	One has to choose appropriate theory for investigation. Theory is a guide post or director to direct the investigation. Problem can be grounded strongly in the backdrop of the theory.
Different Dimensions	Writer or investigator has to develop acumen to look at issues from different dimensions. Multidimensionality of the problem could be brought out while investigating the problem.
Assimilate	One has to get into the reading and it should be vast and assimilate the relevant ideas. All complexities have to be received and assimilated. Just like a store house. Enormous ideas one should keep on issues on which you are writing.

Ruminate	Ruminate the issues and their dimensions and continuous rumination bring clarity and direction to the investigator. Continuous rumination will give you new ideas and new perspectives.
Identify the Data	From the theory one has to distill the objectives and hypotheses. From the hypotheses one has to indentify the data to be generated for analysis.
Think of Data Dimension	Based on the hypotheses data dimension and nature have to be identified and classify the data as quantitative and qualitative for precision. This process will enable you to construct appropriate tool for data collection.
Think of tools of Data Collection	Appropriate tools have to be used to collect relevant data. To collect data conventional tools can be used or one can innovate tools and they can be used for data collection. At present a large number of newer tools have been evolved to collect data in social science research.
Analysis	Collected data have to be analysed and data analysis tools have to be identified. Tools have to be chosen according to the nature of the data collected.

IX
Selection of Topic

Most pressing problem in the society	If anyone takes an issue which is current, pressing and critical, one can get quick visibility. Socially relevant and contextually relevant issues to be selected to draw the attention of everyone towards you.
Most complicate problem but the society expects solution	If anyone takes a much complicated topic he/shc can draw the attention of the whole society. If you are in a position to identify solution to the problems you will get name quickly.
Contextually relevant	Contextually relevant problems have to be selected for investigation and writing. By writing articles and books on contextual problems and issues, you will be known immediately and widely.
Either it brings solution or gives new dimension to the existing knowledge	The investigation brings either solution to a problem through analysis or it brings newer dimension to the existing knowledge on the area. In such a way problems have to be selected for investigation and writing.
Data should be available	Data should be available within the manageable limit of the scholar. The selection of problem should be based on the availability of materials.

Doable within your research of resources	The whole research exercise should be manageable within the resource limit of the scholars or researchers. The researchers should not find difficulty in resource management.

X
Bringing Clarity

Read Encyclopaedia on basic concepts	In social science research on any issue the first scholar has to consult the social science encyclopaedia. A beginner will get clarity and understanding of the concepts only from Encyclopaedia.
Read basic books referred in the Encyclopaedia on the basic concepts	Encyclopaedia will guide the scholar as to what are all the books to be read by the scholars for furthering his/her understanding.
Read Research Methodology books for select appropriate tools for Data Collection and *Data Analysis*	There are certain basic research methodology books which have to be read by the researchers. Fred. N. Kerlniger "*Foundation of Behavioural Research*". Abraham Kalpam "*Conduct of Inquiry*" and Enernst Nagel "*Structure of Science*". The research methodology kit brought out by Sage for social science research methodology will be much useful for the scholars in social science.
Read books on theory to get clarity and guidance to do research	A researcher can get M.Phil. and Ph.D. degree without going through theoretical foundations. But they cannot establish their grip over the subject without reading theory. Hence, theory is fundamental for social science research. Scholarly writings require theoretical discussions.

XI
Clarity on

To your Problem

The whole research project will be easy if the problem is precisely formulated. One has to take adequate time to formulate a research problem. In order to increase rigour in writing, problem formulation will be precise.

To your Questions

Research questions should be focused, and should be made precise, simple and direct. The research questions have to be seen in the backdrop of a theory. There should be direct link between problem and questions and hypotheses and theory.

To your Concepts

Once problem is formulated and research questions are precisely posited, the concepts used in the investigation have to be defined with adequate clarity. Abstractness have to be simplified and made operational. Operationalization is the most important part of the research exercise.

To your Approaches

While selecting an approach or approaches the researcher has to keep in mind that which is the most suitable approach which will bring solution to the problem and give needed input for knowledge generation. Approach will enable you to analyse the problem more clearly and easily.

To your tools of Data Collection

Data collection tools are so important. They should have the capacity to generate the needed data for the project. They need not be

(contd.)

conventional or traditional. Researcher can devise new tools also for data collection. By your experience you can do lot of innovations in data collection tools.

To your Data Analysis

By consulting statisticians more suitable tools of analysis have to be fixed and through computer data can be classified and analysed as packages are loaded in computers. Because of the technology data analysis can be made very easily. Data generating tools have to be constructed in the backdrop of data analysis tools.

XII
Take an Issue

Relevant to the Society	While selecting a problem for analysis and writing, the scholar has to select more socially relevant issues as it will attract more stakeholders, and it will draw the attention of policy maker, media and opinion makers.
Relevant to the Context	To get the attention of the readers, contextual problems have to be taken for analysis. As contemporary problems are much complicated. It will draw the attention of everyone.
Relevant to the Theme	There are certain research areas or themes identified by the funding and policy agencies and they are to be taken for investigations for getting adequate resource and thereby one can contribute a lot.
Relevant to the Policy	If research investigations are akin to policy matters of government, research will draw the attention of the policy makers and opinion makers. Academics can be invited for idea generation for policy input.
Relevant to the Decision	Your problem should be more relevant to a decision which was taken or the decision which is going to be taken in state legislatures National parliament. It may be related to the impact of the decisions or expected outcome of the decisions. It would attract the attention of the publisher from sales perspective.

Relevant to the Agencies	There are agencies or institutions involved in development activities, decision making and policy making. They in fact identify certain areas which are to be investigated. For instance the Ministry of Panchayati Raj has identified certain areas for research investigation. Thus, scholars can take such issues for investigation and get funds from them.
Relevant to the Publisher	Book publishing companies invite manuscripts for publication on certain areas. If these invitations are falling in our specialization we can work on those areas. There are certain publishers always invite quality manuscripts. If we are in a position to produce quality manuscript, publishing is not a problem.
Relevant to the Journal	Articles can be written for specialized journals. According to the needs of the journals articles have to be prepared. There are specialised journals focus on specific themes. Even areas are given well in advance and the scholars have to prepare quality scripts.
Relevant to the areas of specializations	One has to do all research activities in a area of specialization. Continuously by doing so you can emerge as a specialist. If you are a specialist you will be getting adequate invitation to write articles and books.

XIII
Mind Mapping

Mind mapping is an exercise to be done by the researchers. It is a model exercise and by which researchers have to extract ideas from mind. When researchers get ideas from mind, a map has to be created by putting all the ideas. The whole mapping should look like a tree. The tree has main ideas, and sub-ideas.

Keep the idea at the centre of the Mapping Tree	For mind mapping one has to create a tree like structure on a paper. Main stem is the main theme. Sub-themes are branches. From the sub-themes many themes have to be developed and they are further braches of the tree.
Write the major aspects	Initially major aspects of the theme have to be written on the tree. The scholar has to think deep into the subject and bring the major themes as branches. In the succeeding pages you can see the exercises in the form of tree.
For each major aspect bring sub-ideas and attach with mapping tree	In each major aspect the scholar has to discuss the detailed issues and bring all the points in the tree as sub-branches of the tree. Once mind mapping is over a full-fledged tree will be on the paper. The tree is the basic note and by which you can develop your theme for writing.
From sub-idea to minute ideas and details one has to go	The scholar has to work on minute details of the sub-themes and they are to be brought out as further branches of the sub-themes.

Likewise the idea tree grows

By developing new ideas, the theme tree has to be developed. It is presented here. By seeing the idea tree in the following pages researchers can develop idea tree for their topics.

XIV
Brain Storming Rules

Write every idea on your paper	All ideas irrespective of their relevance have to be written on a paper. Whether ideas put on the paper are relevant or irrelevant they are to be in paper for your consideration. Before you complete the process you should not look back.
Don't control your thought process	Once your thought is stimulated, on a theme, you should not put any control over your thought. It should come as stream and in such a way mind has to be prepared.
Don't make judgements on your ideas	While writing, do not make judgement or analysis. Try to bring all ideas to paper. It should be a non-stop exercise.
Don't edit during that stage	Do not touch the idea and allow your thought to flow ideas. Analysis and editing have to come later. Allow your mind to go far and further to bring ideas.
Bring as much as ideas	Exhaust all ideas; all relevant ideas have to be poured on the paper. The ideas may not be useful for that write up. But it can help elsewhere.

XV
Brain Storming

Keep the idea or problem at the centre	Keep the main idea at the centre of your thinking. For your further problem flash has to come from the main ideas. It should be kept as focus light.
Look at the problem from different perspectives	The problem has to be looked at from different perspectives. If you have a vast reading the central problem could be seen from varied perspectives.
Look at the problem from different dimensions	Each problem has its own dimensions and the dimensions have to be brought out. Your mind should be in a position to indentify the dimensions.
Build on arguments	From the perspectives and the dimensions arguments have to be developed. From the arguments and explanations alone inferences could be drawn.
Support evidence	For all arguments interpretations and explanations, evidences have to be built and cited. Evidence based arguments and explanations will increase the rigour of your write-up.
Derive inferences	From the explanations and interpretations inferences have to be derived. All the inferences should be directly related to the questions raised in the beginning as research questions.

Derive conclusion from inferences	From the inferences conclusion has to be drawn. The conclusion should be directly linked to the statement of the problem.

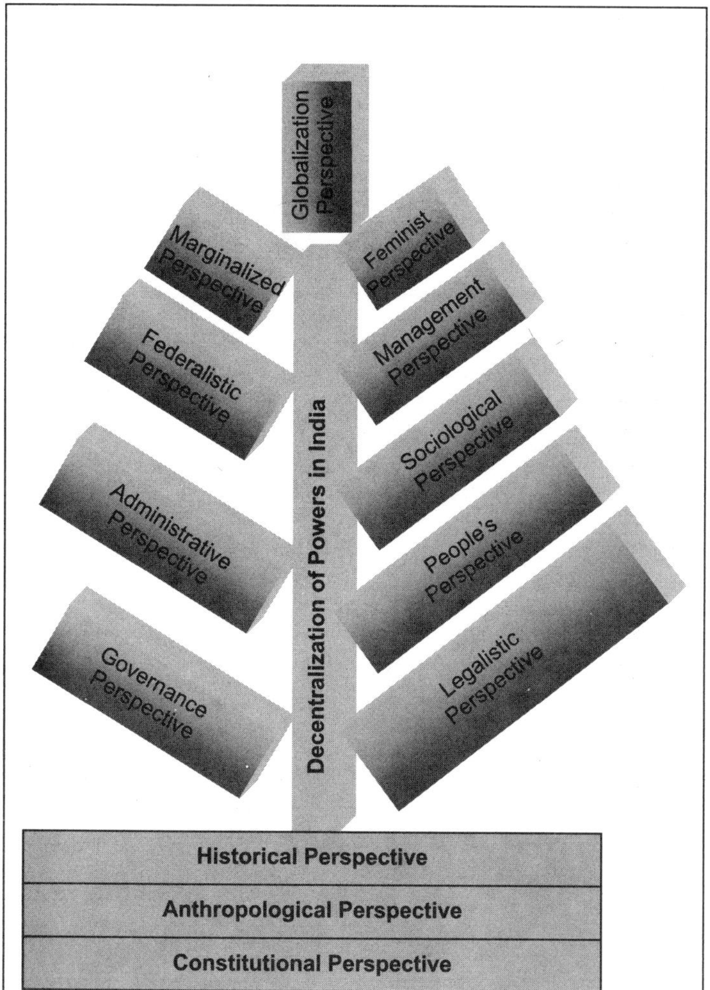

Brain Storming

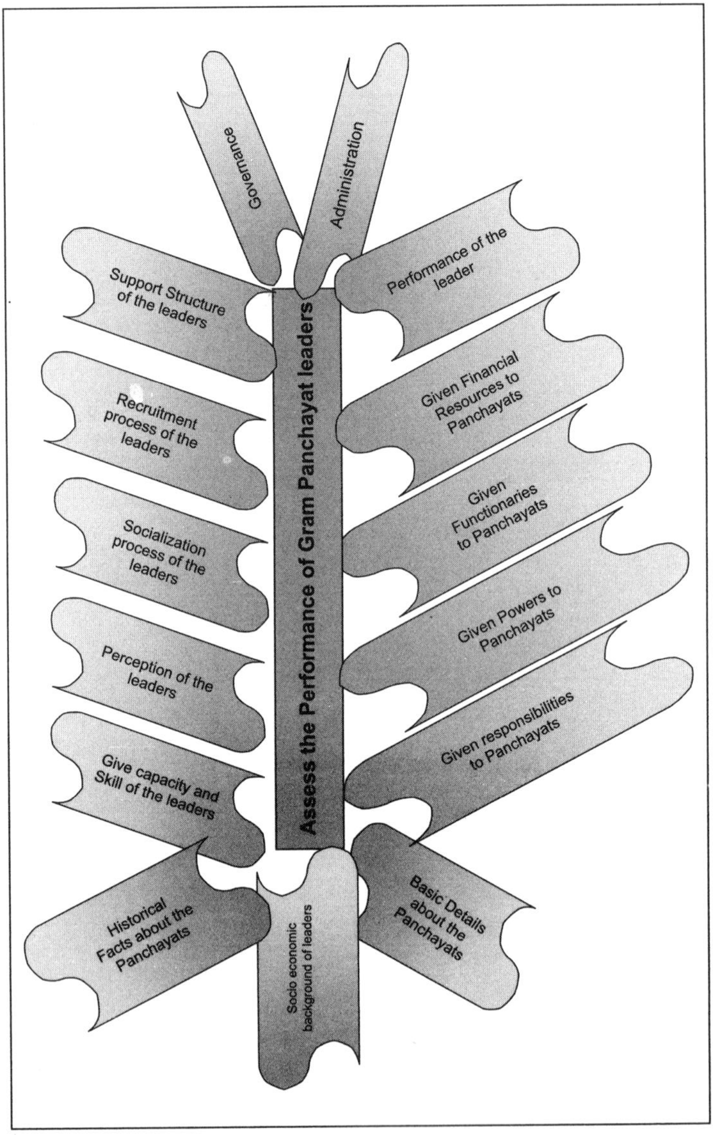

Illustration

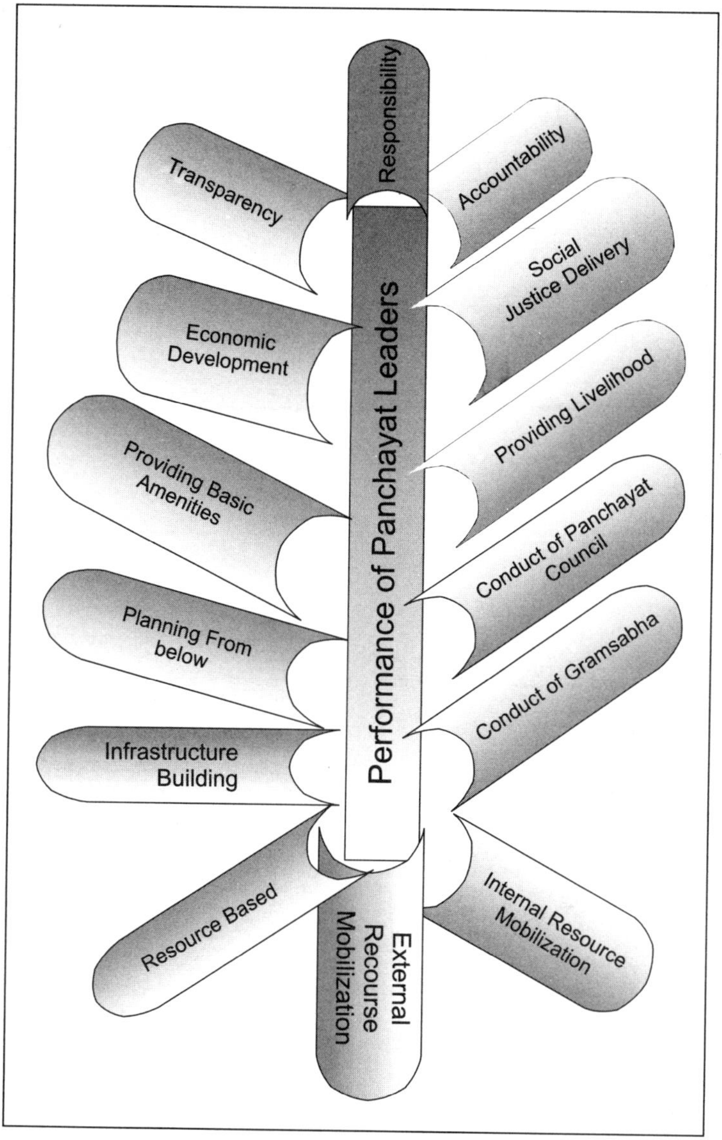

Illustration

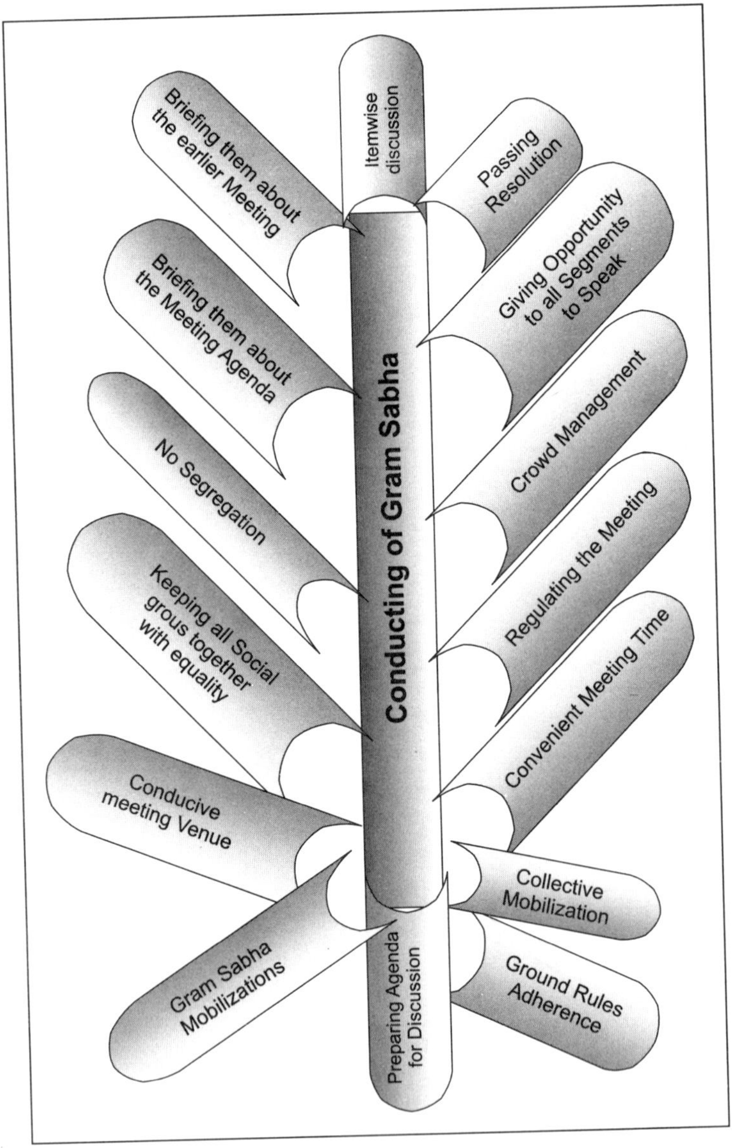

Illustration

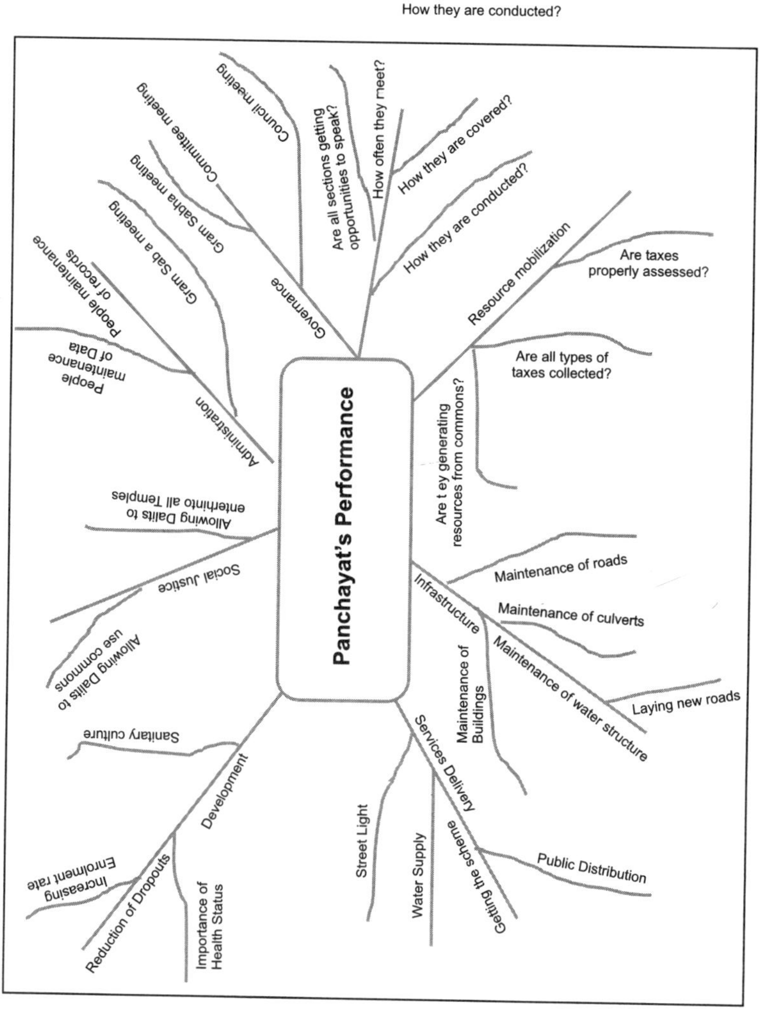
How they are conducted?
Panchayat's Performance
Governance
Council meeting
Committee meeting
Gram Sabha meeting
Gram Sab a meeting
Are all sections getting opportunities to speak?
How often they meet?
How they are covered?
How they are conducted?
Resource mobilization
Are taxes properly assessed?
Are all types of taxes collected?
Are t ey generating resources from commons?
Administration
People maintenance of records
People maintenance of Data
Social Justice
Allowing Dalits to enterhinto all Temples
Allowing Dalits to use commons
Infrastructure
Maintenance of roads
Maintenance of culverts
Maintenance of Buildings
Maintenance of water structure
Laying new roads
Development
Sanitary culture
Increasing Enrolment rate
Reduction of Dropouts
Importance of Health Status
Services Delivery
Street Light
Water Supply
Getting the scheme
Public Distribution

Ideal Tree

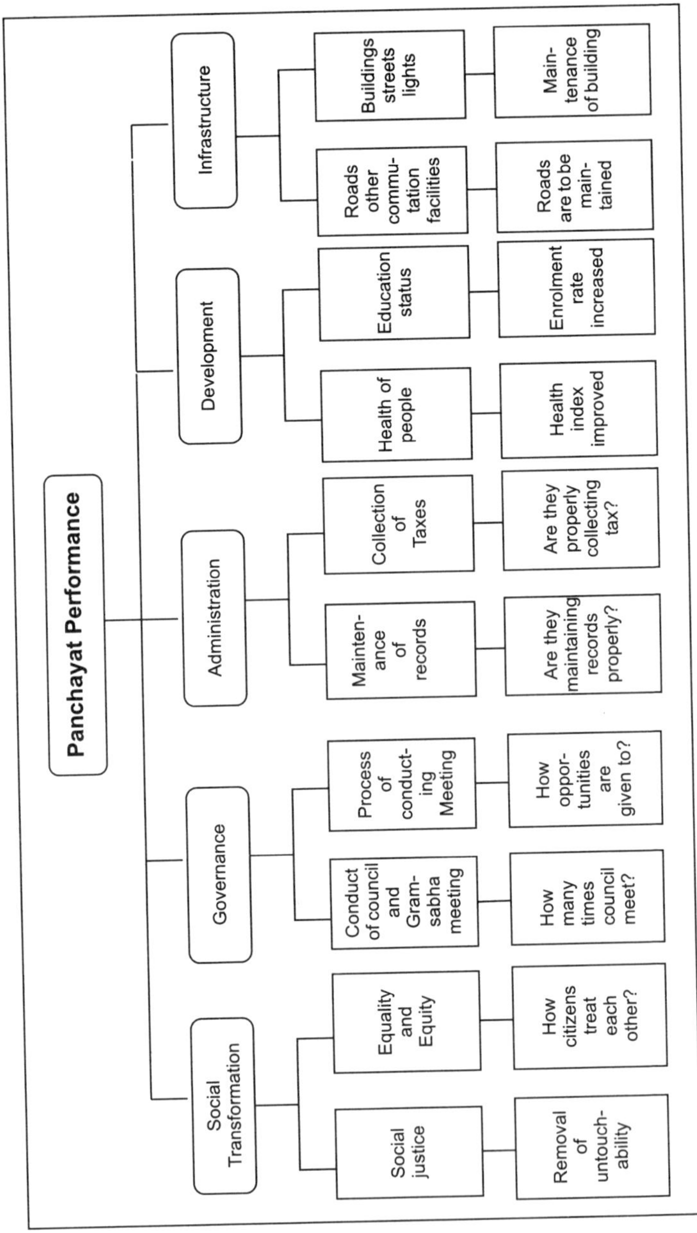

Pasting Sticker Based on Mind Mapping

XVI
Base Writing

Once mind mapping is over	Full of ideas but they are not well organized. All the ideas have to be grouped into different segment and order them.
Write chapters – Elaborate and Complete	Take a branch from the tree, make an analysis and write it as a chapter or a section. Here the scholar has to elaborate each and every idea and complete it.
Reread	Every written chapter is to be reread. After completing the chapters, keep it for a few days. Then you read. You can notice the mistakes. They are to be removed.
Remove unwanted	While mind mapping exercise was on mind brought ideas. All ideas may not relevant and hence you have to remove irrelevant points, ideas from the chapters.
Edit it	In order to bring readability, you have to edit it properly. Language style has to be maintained and it should be kept in tack.
Finalize	From every aspect of the framework of the thesis, book or article, the script has to be seen. From problem statement to conclusion every aspect has to be thoroughly seen.

XVII
Rapid Writing

Allocate time	It should be for three hours or two hours. A suitable time has to be fixed. Depending on the topic, required time has to be fixed for this exercise.
Undisturbed	During the writing time there should not be any disturbance from any side. Your mind should be in peace and tranquility.
In a calm atmosphere	It should not be a noisy place. Absolutely place should provide calm atmosphere and you should be in such a place. It can be in your house or in a garden or in your library or in a small room.
Mostly in night or early morning	Early morning from three thirty to six thirty is a fine time for rapid writing. This is based on my experience. Any time suitable to you has to be fixed.
Allow your mind to go deep	Your thinking process should be elevated to higher level. You have to be deep in your thinking. It should not be in periphery. Surface analysis will not help you to write research articles.
Till you complete don't move out	You should not move out from the place and equally you should not move out from the thought. Be in your thought as you are in meditation.

Don't close your pen	Opened pen should be in your hand till the process is over. Your pen should not be closed as it gives signal to your mind. You should be in higher consciousness level.
Have a finished product	You get some material out of the process and that material is a base material. Based on that material you can develop further. It will help you to develop base material.

XVIII
Rapid Writing for Popular Writing

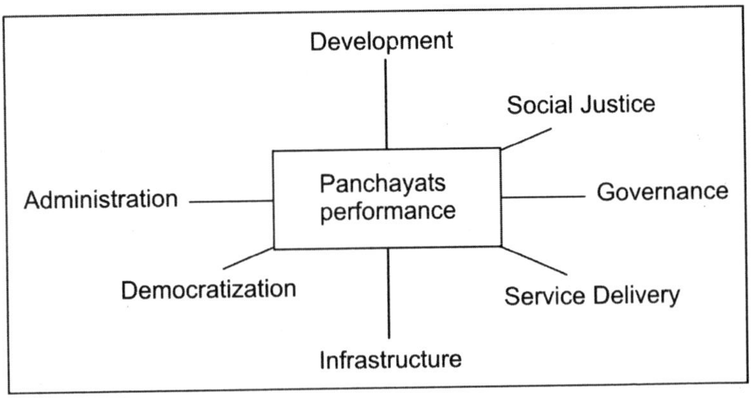

The above is an example for popular writing. Rapid writing exercise can be done for writing popular article for magazines. When you take a subject for writing, go deep into the issues. If you touch in periphery it will become an essay. For example, assuming that you are writing an article on Panchayati Raj, it should be on any one of the issues connected with Panchayat as shown above.

XIX
Managing Time

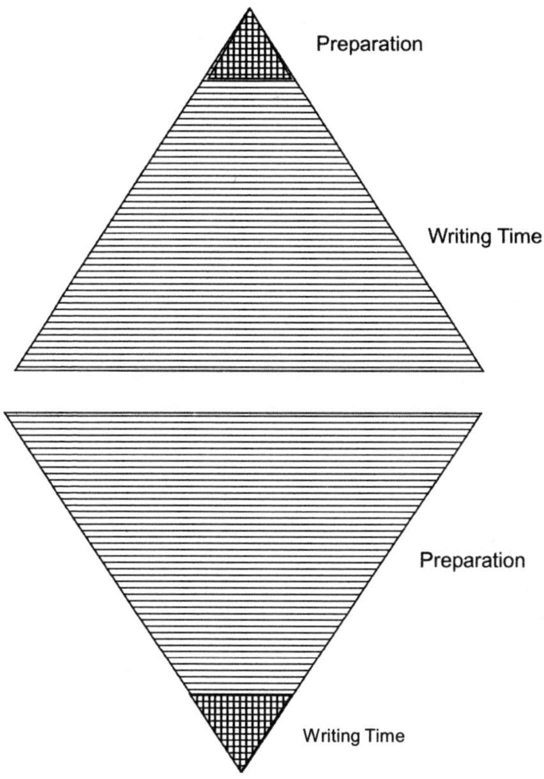

Many of the occasion's researchers have developed aspiration to do research and write continuously. Some will write immediately and struggle. A few take mere time for preparation first and finally, they write. They take a little time for writing the article or report. If you are a professional, you have to take more time for preparation and then you can take a little time for writing.

XX
Basic Writing Rules

Sentence to Sentence connection	There should be an organic link between one sentence to another sentence. Idea link should be between sentences. Logically sentences have to be connected.
Paragraph to Paragraph connection	What has been described and explained in one paragraph should have logical link with the next paragraph. There should be an ideational link between one paragraph to another paragraph.
Section to Section connection	When a section is completed the idea of the above section should be linked with the next section of the chapters. Thematically sections are divided and the sections should have logical connections.
Chapter to Chapter connection	Above logic has to be followed for chapters also. There should be logical and sequential connection between chapters. The whole writing should be like a story telling.

XXI
Research Report

Introduction	To write a research report a brief general introduction has to be given for the whole issue. In this part why this issue has to be probed is to be stated. Importance of the issue has to be stated here.
Problem	Precisely the problem to be investigated should be stated. The whole problem has to be stated in a more focused way. There should not be any ambiguity in the problem formulation.
Research Questions	The research problem has to be broken into different research questions. All the questions have to be directly linked to the problem.
Survey of Literature	The problem selected for investigation has to be justified through extensive review of literature. The gap in knowledge has to be identified and justified through survey of literature.
Indentify the Research Gap	In the existing body of knowledge what are the gaps to be filled have to be identified. The gaps can be filled either through this study or through series of studies.

Objectives and Hypotheses	From the theory objectives have to be formulated and from the objectives hypotheses have to be deduced. Basically theory will guide the researcher to formulate hypotheses.
Problem in the Backdrop of the Theory	For a sound and deep investigation theoretical background is the basic ingredient. Theory is the lighthouse which will shed light on the path of investigation.
Data collection tool formulation	Once the objectives and hypotheses have been formulated from the theory, variables have to be identified. To collect and analyse the data tools have to be finalized.
Data Collection	Precisely needed and relevant data have to be collected through the tools finalized. Professional way of data collection will make the job easier. You need not to collect unwanted data that will waste your time.
Data Analysis	If the data collection tools are constructed with precision, data analysis will be much easier and it can be done through machine. Since data collection and data analysis tools are finalized precisely data analysis becomes easy.
Results and Discussions	Once researcher gets results from data analysis, the results have to be explained and interpreted. It requires full understanding of the theory and the results. It gives answer to all the problems.
Conclusion	From the interpretations and explanations of the result of data analysis, one has to draw conclusion. Interpretation and explanations are based on the inferences while drawing conclusion one has to look at the problem.

Policy Recommendation	From conclusion researchers have to make policy recommendation. It will lead to action. To do policy advocacy, policy recommendations are very essential.

XXII
Popular Article

Take an issue	For popular article to be published in the magazines, take an appropriate and socially relevant issue for writing. It should be focused and precise. One to attract the readers.
Project it	Try to project why it should be explored and how this issue is so important. Contextually it has to be projected. Significance of the issue has to be highlighted.
State it clearly	When the issue is stated, it has to be stated unambiguously. Precision and focus should be maintained while stating the issue. With adequate clarity it has to be protected.
See it objectively	The issue has to be seen very objectively. While analyzing the issue high standard of objectivity has to be maintained.
Look at it from different dimensions	The issue has to be seen from the different dimensions and perspectively. A multidimensional analysis will bring volume of truth on the issues.
Analyse if based on the data	Any analysis should be based on data and evidences. Data have to be analysed. Empirical analysis requires data and they should be with exact precision.
Derive the result	From the data analysis results have to be obtained. Appropriate tools have to be used for data analysis.

Explain and interpret it	Whatever results obtained from the analysis, they are to be explained and interpreted. While interpreting the results explanatory evidences have to be used to support the arguments.
Draw the findings	From the base arguments, explanations and interpretations of the results, findings have to be drawn.
Draw the conclusion	From the findings conclusions are to be drawn. Conclusion has to be in relation to the problem stated.
From the introduction to interpretation and explanation, statements have to be substantiated by citing references	From the vast readings of subjects one will provide adequate arguments for interpreting the results of the analysis of data. All the arguments are to be substantiated.

XXIII
Write Up Can be

A small popular article	Article with 800 to 1000 words on a particular issue meant for ordinary citizens of the country. It can be for a newspaper or a magazine.
A serious thematic popular article	Article on a serious theme with 1000 to 2500 words. It is meant for opinion makers. It is with a view to generate discussion.
A research article	A research article which can be for a referred journal with the format given by the journal. It is with a purpose of adding new knowledge with the existing.
A monograph	A monograph is also a serious research write-up on a theme and it is neither an article nor a book.
A working paper	A working paper will be on an issue or a problem which generates new ideas and identifess new methodological nuances.
A book	A book will be on a theme and it will also like a thesis.

XXIV
Structure of Any Write-Up

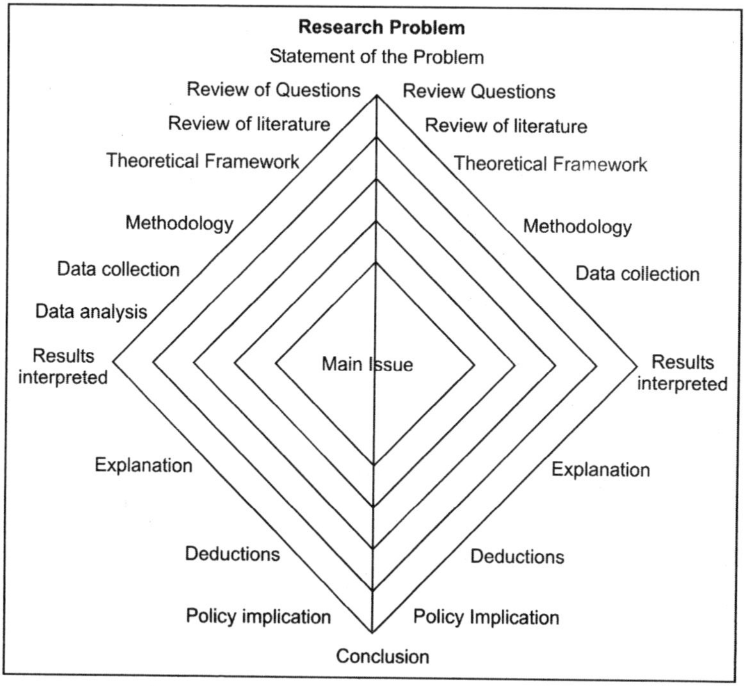

Findings and Conclusion

The whole write-up should start from a problem and it will be expanded in the process of finding answer to the problem and it will be reduced just like the diagram shown above. From statement of the problem expansion goes further and further once results are obtained from the analysis deduction has to be made. From the process of deduction conclusion has to be arrived. Conclusion will touch upon the problem. The whole write-up will end in the point where investigation starts.

XXV
Building Blocks

Whether it is an article or a book or a monograph or a working paper, it has to grow like the building blocks shown in the following picture. It has to grow from statement of the problem. In the same way it has to be reduced from interpretation to conclusion.

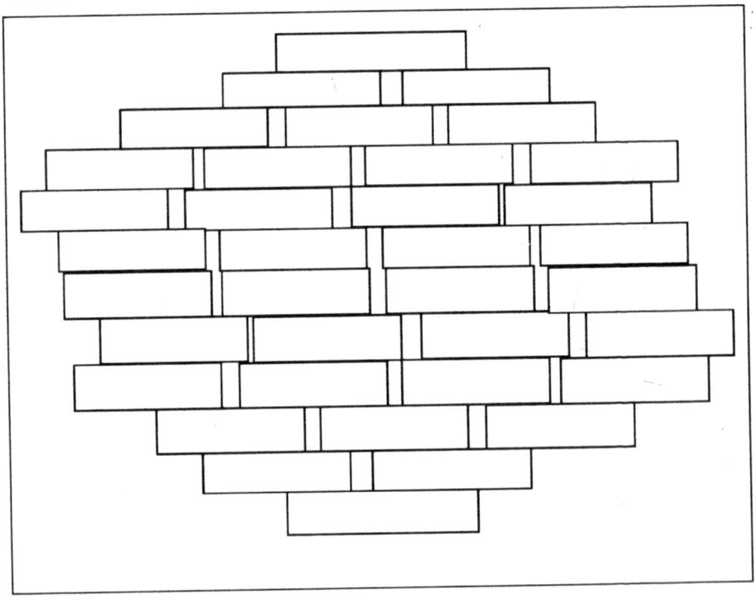

XXVI
Resource Management

Identifying the agency for support	When we take up issue or theme for serious writing it needs resources and for which we have to identify the agency. Identifying the agency is the first step.
Priority of the support agency	We have to match the priority area which we have chosen and the priority area of the funding agencies.
Assessing the resource requirements	One should be able to estimate the expenditure involved in carrying out the research in the chosen theme.
Government agencies	At present all government agencies are giving resources to pure research and action research.
Donor agencies	Several donor agencies are financially supporting research activities. Most of the donor agencies are interested in action research.
Corporates	Corporate under corporate social responsibility invests money on action research on the critical issues of development. Sometimes they have chosen areas we have to work on them.
Contractual agencies	There are certain contractual agencies which get huge resource for many development activities and of which one is research.

Business firm	Business organizations for their own advantage give liberally resources for research. That research activity is related to their business.
Government Departments	Government departments are giving huge resources for research both pure and action. One has to find out the departments which are suitable for our proposal.

XXVII
Drafting

First draft is Comprehensive Draft	The Scholar has to draft his/her thesis or report or book extensively and comprehensively in the beginning. Nothing should be left out. In such a way it should be made as a comprehensive draft.
It should be the base document	The first draft should be inclusive document. It should be rough but base document is subjected to perfection. It can be pruned, revised, redrafted and altered.
It should be in the computer separately	Since the scholar has to improve the base document, it should be kept separately in computer. Because when we need some points at a later stage, we can make use of the base documents.
Compare all corrections with the base document	When we correct the report or document, it has to be compared with the base document every time. By doing so we can see the improvement.
Improvement can be easily seen	See the improvements in research methodology, style of arguments, rigour in writing, tenour of the description and presentation. Finalization has to done after all the corrections are over.

XXVIII
Referencing

There are different types of referencing numbering in the text and putting the reference at the bottom of every page

There are different types of references used by scholars depending in their requirement. It varies from journal to journal.

Examples

Putting the details of source in brief in the text itself in bracket and finally putting all the references at the end.

> With regard to GS the first study on Mandal system (Aziz, Nelson and Babu, 1996:153-54) brought out that GS meetings were held regularly in the first two years, but in due course their number and that of villages where the meetings were held gradually declined. A study of poverty alleviation during three regimes of panchayats i.e. mandal period, administrators' period and the immediate regime after 73rd Amendment brought out that "in the initial enthusiasm GSs were held at least during the initial two years, and citizens were given opportunity to participate in decision-making; during the regime of administrators, a void had been created between citizens and officers as GS meetings were not held regularly and people's participation in decision making had become a thing of the past. Touts and middlemen

Examples

For books giving reference I either one of the above. In certain books at the end of each and every chapter notes and references are given. In certain books at last reference will be given chapterwise.

> In this tense atmosphere the verdict of death passed by Tribunal on Bhagat Singh, Sukhdev and Rajguru virtually shook the nation. In a speech at Allahabad on October 12, 1930, five days after the award of sentence of death, Jawaharlal Nehru said, "Whether he agreed with Bhagat Singh or nor, his heart was full of admiration for the courage and self-sacrifice of Bhagat Singh. A man of his type is exceedingly rare. If the Viceroy expects us to refrain from admiring this wonderful courage and high purpose behind it, he is mistaken. Let him ask his own heart what he would have felt if Bhagat Singh had been an Englishman and acted for England".[2]

XXIX
Reference Purposes

To support the Statement made	When statements of others are used in the text within quote, reference has to be cited.
To support the argument made	Sometimes we draw only arguments and mideas and not verbatim statement and for which references have to be given.
To support the explanation	When you make explanation in the process, we draw points from others to amplify and for which also reference has to be cited.
It may be in the form of book	References can be taken from book written and edited by scholars. In such case name of the author, name of the publisher, year of publication, page number have to be written as per the guidelines stipulated in the manual.
It may be in the form of article	Reference can be taken from journal articles. Reference has to be given as per the manual. We follow.
It may be in the form of data	Sometimes we take data from the books, reports and other compiled proceedings. They are also to be cited.
It may be in the form of reports	On many occasions we quote reports and take points from the reports. The report details have to be cited.

It may be in the form of Official declarations	Often we quote official declarations also. They are to be quoted, from the basic document either government orders or newspapers.

XXX
Writing

It is not one stroke writing	Writing article, monograph, working paper, book, and occasional papers can be written over for a period of time. It is not a work of a day or two. It will take a week or a month or two.
You have different pieces of writing	Periodically we are writing. May be on a same theme or different themes. A writer or a researcher should have the habit of writing continuously. Hence, they can be compiled at a later stage and make them into books.
Integrate all the Writing into one Part as Article or Monograph or Book	Integrate thematically all the writings to make an article or monograph or a book or part of all.
Parts of the Monograph	Any writing can be incorporated into a Monograph if it is relevant to the theme of the monograph.
Parts of the Book	Any writing can be incorporated into a book, if it is relevant for the theme of the book.
Parts of the Thesis	Any writing can be incorporated into a thesis, if it is relevant to the thesis. Scholars publish papers when they are in Ph.D. programme. When they submit their thesis all published articles integrated into their thesis.

Basically the writer and researcher has to write continuously.

Nothing is a waste.

Write and keep it.

XXXI
Framework of Article

General introduction	Write a very brief general introduction about the theme on which you are going to write. While doing, you have to state the importance and significance of the theme or issue on which you are writing.
Topic introduction	Specifically what you want to touch upon has to be clearly stated. The issue on which you are going to write has to be clearly stated.
Background of the issue	When you write you must state clearly the background of the issue. It may be a historical setting.
Theoretical underpinnings	If you are able to look at the issue in the backdrop of the theory, your writing will be very sound.
Methodological nuances	Methodological nuances have to be specified clearly as how you are collecting and analyzing data with what perspective have to be stated.
Presentation of results of the analysis	With adequate clarity results have to be presented.
Interpretation and Explanation	The results of the analysis have to be interpreted and explained in the backdrops of the theory which you have chosen.

Relating the results with theory	Each and every major result have to be linked with the theory and they are to be explained in detail with adequate clarity.
Deriving inferences from the analysis of results	Inferences have to be derived from the arguments, interpretations and explanations.
Deriving the conclusion from the inferences	From the inferences conclusion has to be drawn.
Way forward	From the conclusion where we want to go has to be decided.
Areas for further probing references	From the conclusion one has to explore the new areas for further investigation.

XXXII
Style of Writing

Audience oriented	An Author gets recognition only because of his readers. Who is his/her reader has to be decided. Accordingly he has to decide the style of writing.
It should be simple	Simple way of writing will always attract more number of people. One can follow some models like Nehru.
Easy to understand	It should be written in such a way that everyone should understand easily and assimilate quickly.
It should be enjoyable	While giving idea the style of writing should make the reader more enjoyable.
Flow should be in fact through out	Just like water moving from higher to lower, flow should be there in the writing and force should be there in writing.
Unless it is for scientific journal, jargons have to be avoided	If the article is for a professional journal, concepts, concerts and specialized jargons have to be used otherwise simple words have to be used.

XXXIII
Correction and Pruning

Keep the entire writing for few days on your table without reading it	Once drafting is over, you need not read immediately. Give some time to your mind to forget. After a few days, just like a fresher read it as if you are reading the text first time.
Read the article or monograph or book after a period of three to seven days gap	After a gap of few days, just like a fresher read it as if you are reading the text first time. You will find the inadequacies of your writing.
Kindly note the points for correction in the margin of the gaps	While making corrections first where correction has to be made and how it should be made, should be indicated in the side margin of the paper.
Once entire reading is over, start correcting the entire manuscript	Once the entire text is read, you start correcting the text here and there. First reading should be a full reading and it should be done at a stretch.
Carryout the Correction in the Computer	Page-wise see the instruction written on the margin of the script and do carry out the corrections in the text in the computer.
As your colleague or an expert to give independent opinion	When you get independent opinion on your paper from the experts, go through the comments and carry out the corrections if they are agreeable.

Get the opinion, go through, if acceptable do the corrections	Make a thorough analysis of the opinion of the experts and accordingly make corrections if the observations are acceptable.

XXXIV
Instruments for Research Writing

Stick Sticks mind mapping and Brain storming	
Cards — Bibliography card	It is a small card in which you have to write only the details of the Author, title of the book, place of publication, year of publication.
Subject	It should be four times bigger than the Bibliography card and in which you have to write the matter taken from the book or article or monograph, while taking such notes you have to mention Author and book name.
Markers and Highlighters	To read articles and reports—underline the important points.
Pen and Pencil	Free flow pens will enthuse the writer. For correction micro tip pen will be useful. Important sentences have to be underlined by the pencil.

XXXV
What is Needed to a Writer?

Interest in writing	Unless you have developed a passion and interest for writing, writing is not so easy. If you cultivate a habit it becomes a routine. Basic interest is needed.
Vast reading	Vast reading is necessary. One has to read relevant literature on the subject you have chosen for specification.
Deep thinking	Whatever you read from the books, articles, and monographs they are to be assimilated and they are to be comprehended and they are to be processed. It needs a deep thinking.
Deep analysis	While making analysis you have to do it in a penetrating way. It should not be cursory analysis. It should be so solid touching the base of the issues.
Passion	Passion means, it should have connection with your higher self.
Hard work	Unless you work hard you cannot bring this habit of writing in you. Hard work alone makes you to write.
Practice	Writing is a practice. To become a writer you have to develop a practice of writing and it should be done routinely and regularly.

Relevant to the Context	When you take up any issue for investigation and write up, if it is contextually relevant it draws the immediate attention of all. Contextual issues will draw the attention of all segments.
Relevant to the Society	If it is highly relevant to the society that too to the present day it would attract the attention of everyone. You will be the most sought after person.
Excluded, Marginalized, Vulnerable	For example when you take-up the issue of excluded or marginalized it would attract everyone as exclusion and marginalization are key issues confronted by everyone in the society.
Relevant to Policy Domain	If your write-up is relevant to a policy or a decision or a law or allocation of resources it will be of much interest to policy makers.
Relevant to Donors	Some issues would attract the attention of the donor agencies. Donor agencies change their priorities and accordingly they search for institutions to fund for research. If you fall in their category certainly you will be receiving their attention.
Priorities of the Institutions and Organisations	Each and every organization has its own priorities of research area and they are to be pursued by the scholars to get recognition within the institute. Policy makers think of some institutions as they specialise on certain areas. They are known for their excellence.
Relevant to Journals	You have to write articles to the requirements of the journal. When journal priority areas and themes are known, you have to concentrate on the same. But do not venture into new areas for the sake of writing.

Relevant to your Area of Specialization

One has to concentrate more on his/her own specialization instead of roaming around. If you are strict to your own domain after a few years of writing, writing will be easy and joyful.

Break new Grounds

If you are breaking new ground, you have to write article or monograph or book on the new area. It will be path breaking. It will be on some subjects or issues or even in methodology.

Street Vendors

Vettiyans

Manual Scavengers

Drainage Cleaners

Maid Servants

Mortuary workers

Functioning of PDS

Hospices not
Old Age Homes

Waste Management

Development Displacement

Development Rehabilitation

Climate Change

Earth Warming

Global Warming

XXXVI
Graphs, Charts, and Diagrams

Graphs, Charts, and Diagrams are the powerful devices to explain the complicated details in the simple terms. Depending on the requirement they are to be used by the scholar while writing the report or article or monograph or book. By seeing the charts and diagrams one can easily understand the trend or level.

Column chart

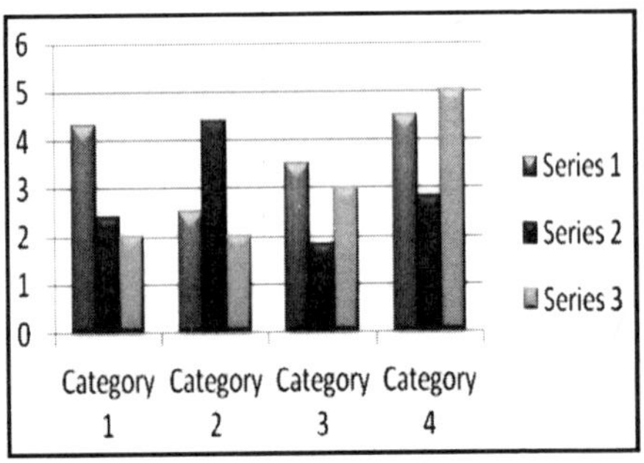

Line chart

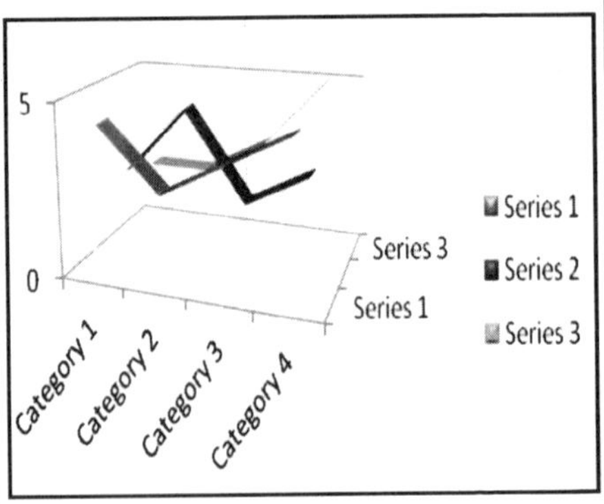

Pie Chart	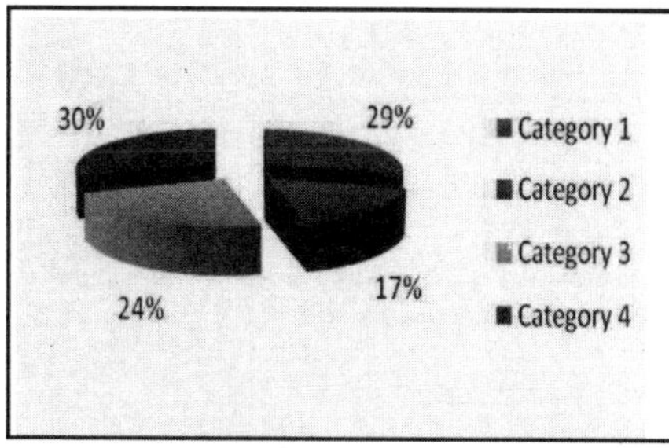
Area Graph Chart	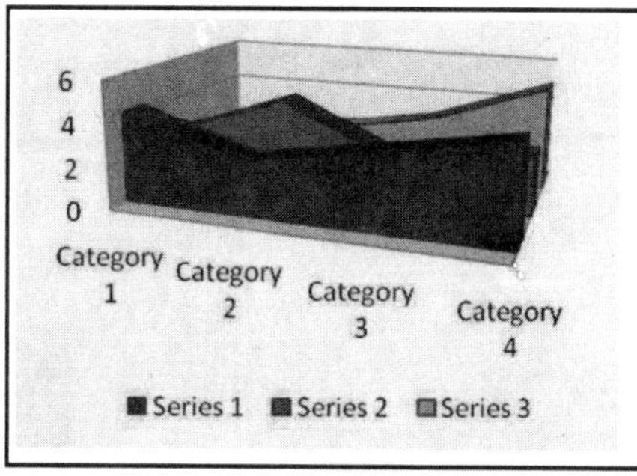
Bar Chart	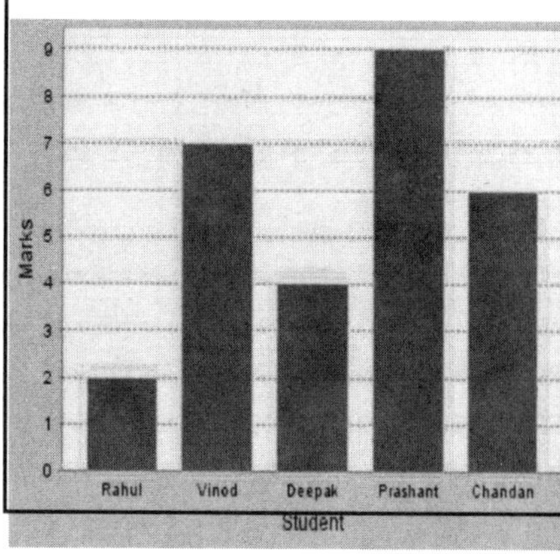

Doughnut	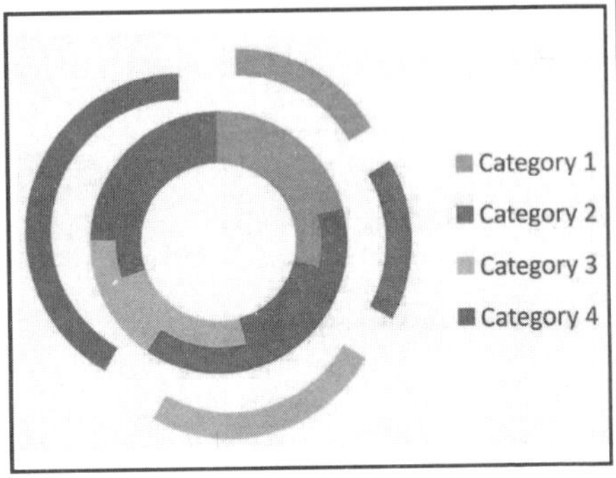
Surface Chart	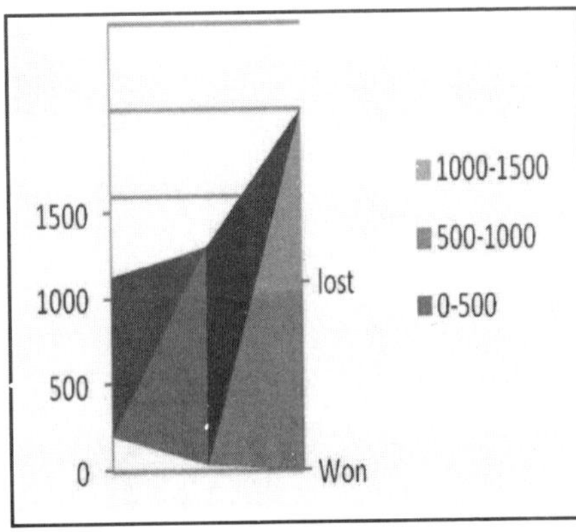
Bubble Chart	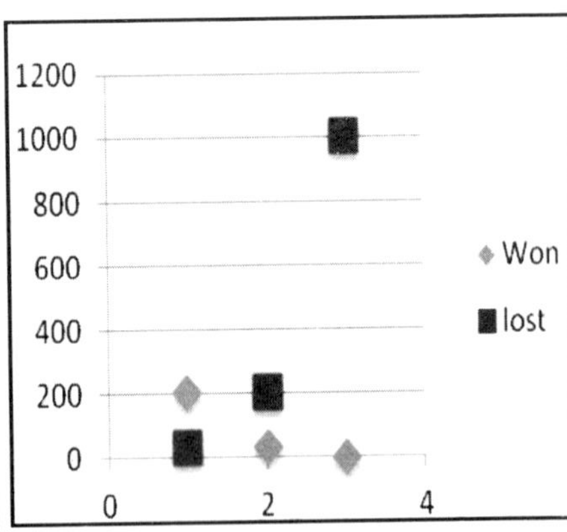

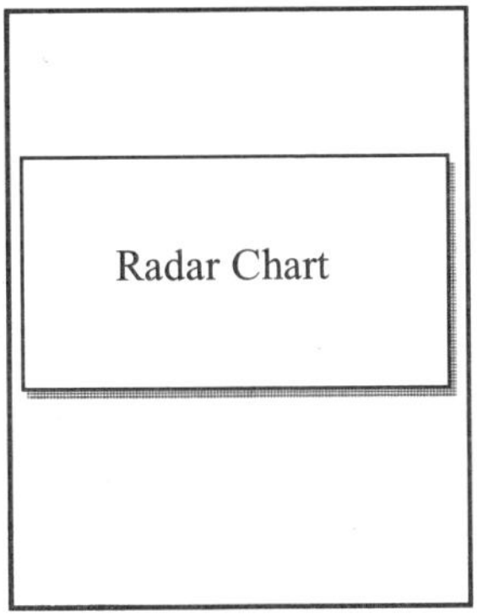
Radar Chart

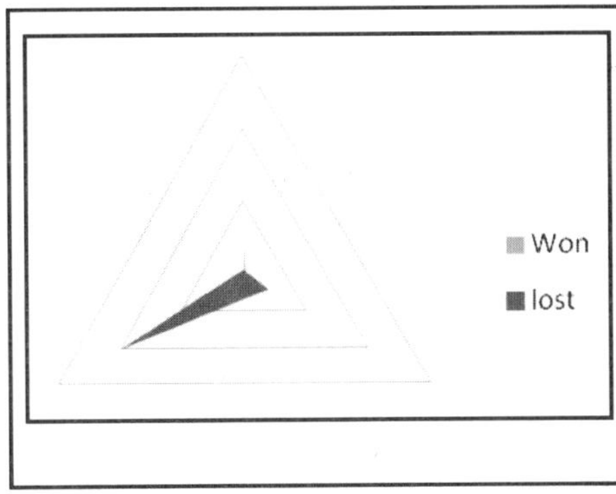
Won
lost

XXXVII
Lens to Check

Once the draft is over whether it is an article or monograph or book or report one has to keep the following in the backdrop to peruse the document whether it is in correct form:

Lens to check	Focus	Description
Lens to check	Subject Focus	The scholar has to check carefully whether the focus of the subject is maintained throughout the write up.
	Reader Focus	The scholar has to see whether write up maintains the reader's focus. Whether it will reach the targeted reader.
	Stimulus Focus	The scholar has to check whether the write-up is stimulating the thinking and reading of the stakeholder.
	Direction Focus	The write-up should not lose the direction. It has to be seen whether the direction is maintained.
	Communication Focus	One has to see whether the article communicates clearly to the reader. Communication should be lucid and enjoyable.

XXXVIII
Drafting

While drafting the article or report or book one has to keep the following factors in the backdrop.

Drafting

Tone or Tenor	To communicate your ideas the tone and tenor of the language is more important.
Accuracy	Precision is the need. Accurately you have to make statement. You should not beat around the bush.
Jargon	For popular articles you should not use jargons and for research articles and reports you can use jargons.
Clear	At every level clarity is needed. While writing you should give clarity.
Concise	You should not add pages. Size of the article and report should be small.
Coherent	Cogency and cohence are necessary for any write-up.
Lead Sentence	In every section and chapter the lead sentence has to be highlighted.
Concluding Sentence	Concluding sentences should be written in response to the statement of the problem.

XXXIX
Correction

Corrections are made differently and repeatedly but one has to follow certain basic rules in correction. They are as follows:

Corrections

Content	Content of the article and books has to be corrected carefully and it should be rich and to the point.
Alignment	Alignment of the article and books have to be checked carefully.
Heading	Appropriate headings have to be given. Misleading headings should not be given.
Paragraph	Paragraphs have to be created with some rationales. It is not based on size and space.
Reference	References have to be checked in terms of accuracy and format as stipulated in the manual.
Language	One has to see the language part of the article. It should be simple and communicative powerfully.

XL
Writing

Planning	Before writing the article or book or report or thesis, proper planning is needed. Once it is planned, writing is easy and methodical.
Writing	Consciously the writer has to follow the generic rules which will enable to complete it at the earliest.
Revising	Once writing is over, the same draft has to be revised. Revision has its own methodology. By following the methods, your write-up has to be revised.
Editing	Editing is a technical job. It can be done either by yourself or a professional. Once editing is over again it has to be seen by the author.

Have you Decided to Write?

Yes

Step - I	Choose an area for your specialization.
Step - II	Start reading relevant Literature.
Step - III	While reading the relevant literature whether it is an article or a book or a monograph or a report, review the same and put the review in your computer under the heading review of literature.

Step - IV	While reviewing literature concentrate on two aspects—substantive and methodological.
Step - V	Classify the reviews and put them in different headings.
Step - VI	Read lot of theories on the subject in which you are specializing.
Step - VII	Constantly interact with other colleagues who are specializing on the same area or interact with best experts on this subject through e-mail on the issues which require clarity in few years.
Step - VIII	Once you establish your grip on the subject theoretically and on the substantive aspect, you can easily identify the gaps.
Step - IX	Try to work on the Gap first identify the gap in theory, second identify the gap in methodological nuances and third on the substantative matters of the subject.
Step - X	Try to write on certain themes and put it in a new folder. You can write on themes, methods, substance.
Step - XI write articles	Once you have developed confidence for writing articles some of the journals.
Step - XII Tackle feed back	It your article is returned with comments, take the comments sportively and correct the article and send the same.
Step - XIII Compile the published Article	When you have a few articles published in different journals on a particular area of specialization, compile all the articles into a book form with the permission of the Journal and give it to a publisher for publication.

Now your academic Flight is in a take off stage.

Computer is an Imperative Need

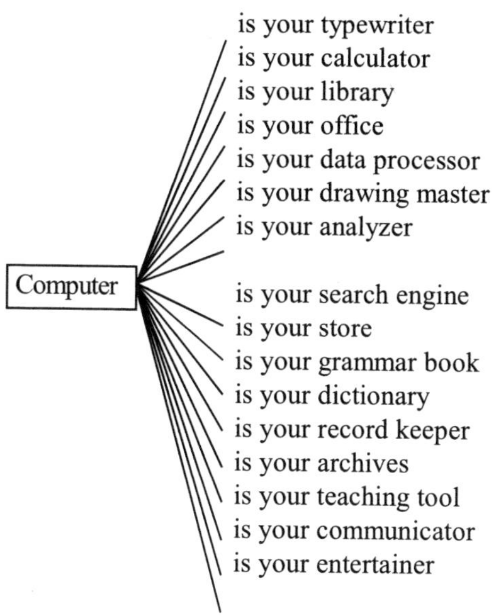

XLI
Get Start

My intension is not to prepare a manual for to the scholars to write a perfect quality article. I have mentioned in the beginning I want more number of teachers in social science disciplines to do research continuously on relevant social issues and get them published. No article or book is complete and perfect. Quality and perfection are relative terms. First one has to write and while writing continuously one can bring quality and perfection. Without jumping into water and drink water, one cannot swim by reading dozens of books on swimming. Teachers in higher learning institutions have to perform three major responsibilities and they are teaching, research and outreach. To excel in teaching one has to excel in research and outreach and *vice versa*. All the three responsibilities have to be carried out by the teachers in higher learning institution. Hence writing is an imperative need and one has to start. One should not wait for perfection.

Let us keep flaming in
our heart in fire
of progress

Index